Revisiting
Hypnosis

Revisiting Hypnosis

by Graham Old

The Principles and Practice of
Post-Hypnotic Re-induction Training
for Anchoring, Post-hypnotic Suggestions
and Inductions

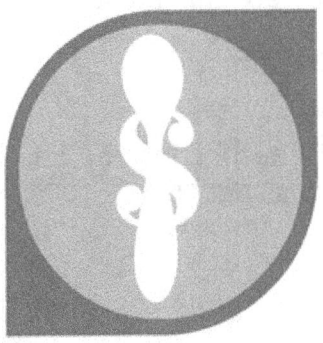

Revisiting Hypnosis

First published 2016 by Plastic Spoon

Acknowledgements

As always, I owe a debt of gratitude to those that I consider my mentors in therapeutic hypnosis - Stephen Brooks, Michael Ellner and Richard Nongard. Each one has had an immeasurable impact on my approach to hypnosis.

I am also nauseatingly grateful to my partner in crime, Jon Old, who continues to direct my focus towards solutions that work in the real world.

All Rights Reserved

Disclaimer

This work is meant as nothing more than an example of one way to carry out post-hypnotic suggestions, re-inductions and anchoring. It offers an approach for consideration, investigation and conversation. This approach is based upon our own clinical studies and is being made public for the purposes of research and development. It is not meant as a replacement for proper training in hypnosis or psychotherapy.

Please be aware that any experimentation with the ideas presented in this document is undertaken at your own risk and responsibility. At all times when practising hypnosis, it is your responsibility to ensure that you comply with the laws, regulations and codes of your home country, region, state or territory.

A Note on Terminology Used

Throughout this text we may use terms such as trance, depth and so on. Please be aware that these terms are merely meant to convey what the subject experiences. At no point are we making any claims as to neuroscientific evidence or endorsing any particular interpretation of hypnosis.

Preface

Revisiting Hypnosis: The Principles and Practice of Post-Hypnotic Re-induction Training is the second book in our *Inductions Masterclass* series.

Our first book, *Mastering the Leisure Induction*, introduced the series and its rather ambitious intention to unpack inductions, whilst simultaneously teaching some of the important principles and skills employed by effective hypnotists. In short, our aim for each book in this series is that they will act as useful introductions to the wider workings of hypnosis by extracting valuable insights from the practice of specific inductions.

When we first stumbled upon the idea for the series, we were genuinely surprised that no one else had beaten us to it. In fact, it remains the case that not only are there very few books which use an induction to teach wider lessons, there are actually very few works which focus on and unpack an individual induction in any real depth. Therefore, our hope that this series will fill a vital gap in the Hypnosis education market is both ambitious and realistic.

The format of this book varies from its predecessor, though the style remains similar. We are again aiming to duplicate the level, detail and quality of information you might receive at a live training. So, we aim to provide in-depth practical information, point to useful theoretical discussions, anticipate questions from 'the Floor' and handle natural diversions and meandering discussions.

Whilst *Mastering the Leisure Induction* primarily focused on Observation and Utilisation, the current work re-introduces the useful concept of Fractionation and demonstrates the practice of Anchoring, whilst offering some thoughts on the theory behind it. As with all of our products and training, our aim here is to point to deep theory through sharing practical knowledge in a refreshingly clear and accessible way.

The PHRIT process is an original creation from howtodoinductions.com and the Brief Hypnosis team.

Contents

Introduction..11

Why Learn PHRIT?..13

The Transcript..23

Anchors & Post-Hypnotic Suggestions.....................33

The Practice of Good Anchoring............................39

The Steps to Good Anchoring...............................43

Unconscious Learned Behaviours...........................51

Collapsing Anchors..59

The Basic Process...69

Breaking it Down..73

Variations & Applications..................................79

Trouble-Shooting and FAQ..................................95

Where Can I Learn More?..................................103

APPENDIX A - Eliciting States.............................109

APPENDIX B - Stacking Anchors...........................115

APPENDIX C - Chaining Anchors..........................117

Bibliography..131

About the Author...135

Introduction

The essence of hypnosis lies in enabling other people to experience a shift in their reality. However, the real art of therapeutic hypnosis is in empowering people to experience that shift so effectively that it remains with them once they return to the "real" world.

One way to achieve such lasting results is to employ post-hypnotic suggestions. Aside from prolonging the effect of suggestions given during hypnosis, post-hypnotic suggestions begin to break down the wall between the hypnotic world and the real world.

The process that we call Post-Hypnotic Re-induction Training, or PHRIT (*pronounced 'fritt'*), began a number of years ago as a simple induction. It grew out of my attempts to develop a fail-safe way to execute re-inductions, to save time in sessions. My thinking had been that I could use a longer induction during my first session and then set-up an anchor to allow me to deliver rapid re-inductions in subsequent sessions.

Over time, my view of inductions changed significantly. As seen in *The Anatomy of Inductions*, I now view the induction as a central part of the entire therapeutic process. So, I am no longer as concerned with increasing the speed of my inductions, or saving time for its own sake. However, what I have seen instead is that there are all kinds of reasons for teaching clients the PHRIT process, not least of which are the therapeutic benefits of teaching self-hypnosis or rapid relaxation.

There have been other positive outcomes from developing the Post-Hypnotic Re-induction Training process. Namely, the many applications that come from employing an approach that is permissive, progressive and empowering. The truth is that there is little that we do in hypnosis that is not, in some sense, reliant on the ability to make lasting suggestions. I am now convinced that the PHRIT process teaches both Hypnotists and their subjects a practical and flexible way to frame effective suggestions that endure beyond the hypnosis session.

I trust that you will find this process as useful as I and my colleagues have. If PHRIT is half as beneficial as my rather biased enthusiasm perceives it to be, then not only do you have in your hands a powerful means of inducing hypnosis - whilst setting-up a re-induction - but you are also about to discover a disarmingly simple and effective means of setting anchors and preparing post-hypnotic suggestions.

Enjoy the journey!

GRAHAM OLD

Why Learn PHRIT?

A Learning Experience

At its core, *Post-Hypnotic Re-induction Training* is a simple yet reliable way to set-up a re-induction. It works, essentially, by helping the hypnotee learn - through experience - how to respond.

I have spoken with a number of new hypnotists who struggled with setting-up re-inductions. In a good proportion of cases, the issue came down to an incorrect presumption on the part of the hypnotist. They had presumed that their client would know what it means to go back into hypnosis, even if it was in a different way to that which they had just been through. Yet, this is far from an easy thing to learn.

Think of it from the client's perspective. You go to see a kind and calm Hypnotherapist who, over time, may subtly and gently lead you into an experience of deep and profound relaxation. In fact, this relaxation is so deep that you had no idea you could experience anything like that. The hypnotist then tells you that whenever he clicks his fingers you will instantly re-enter that state. How on earth are you meant to do that?!

Now, some people *will* find themselves automatically, almost 'subconsciously', carrying out the suggestion given to them. They might not know how they do that, but they do. These are the lucky ones who realised - even if they were not completely aware of it - that their former wonderful experience had happened as a result of suggestions given to them by the Hypnotist. So, the suggestion for re-induction makes perfect sense to them, is accepted implicitly and is carried out effortlessly and automatically.

However, this is not true for everyone. For those less fortunate clients - and their frustrated hypnotists - you may just as well painstakingly teach someone the Waltz and then ask them to Street Dance. They may be aware of a connection between the two, but they will likely have no idea how knowing the one enables them to do the other.

This is where PHRIT is so useful. It works by teaching the client how to respond progressively - and helping them experience the effect along the way. So, when you come to give the final post-hypnotic suggestion, they know precisely what is expected of them and they know that they have it within them to respond appropriately. Just as importantly, they are eager to do so!

For some people, this aspect of PHRIT may seem insignificant. It is more than possible that other hypnotists have stumbled upon similar processes to practically teach their clients how to experience post-hypnotic suggestions and re-inductions. However, for some, this element of the PHRIT framework will be the most useful. Not only does PHRIT teach a new way of carrying out re-inductions, but it potentially teaches both clients and hypnotists a new model of therapeutic hypnosis. The hypnosis session can become one of teaching and coaching, rather than simply perpetuating potentially outdated models of hypnotists bending subjects to their will.

Training Wheels (for Hypnotists)

The previous point discussed the experiential learning aspect of PHRIT for clients. However, it is also a learning tool for hypnotists.

Due to the progressive nature of PHRIT, it is a completely risk-free endeavour for new or nervous hypnotists. Believe me, I know how terrifying it can be when you first test a rapid induction. I also know how awkward, embarrassing and debilitating it can be when the client just stares back at you, unhypnotised and apparently unsure what they should be doing!

PHRIT is perfect for such situations, because as the Hypnotist you never really ask the client to do much more than they are already doing. There is an element of stretching them, but it starts off so permissively that it will feel to them as if you are simply giving them permission to carry on enjoying their relaxation (or whatever 'state' your induction is leading them into). As a practitioner, it really does not need to be any more threatening than the most basic 'pacing and leading' exercise that NLPers will be familiar with.

As such, it is perfect for hypnotists who lack experience in working with post-hypnotic suggestions, or who worry that they lack the confidence to pull off a re-induction. Once the hypnotist has successfully carried out his first PHRIT, he can be confident that he has now learned the steps to carrying out practically any post-hypnotic suggestion. More importantly, so has the client. And, yet, within that process they have also learned so much more.

Fractionation Induction + Deepener

One aspect of PHRIT that seems to be an essential part of what makes it so successful is the intrinsic fractionation. Simply by learning how they will later go into hypnosis, the client has been in and out of that 'state' at least four times. Helpfully, for both us and them, each time they do so, they go in even quicker and deeper.

In fact, this is such a powerful part of the process, that I frequently use PHRIT even if I am not intending to see someone for a second session. That may seem pointless, but the process actually serves as an effective induction, a powerful deepener and a quick and easy lesson in self-hypnosis, all in one. Of course, it is more than a tool for re-inductions and thus also allows me to set-up anchors and/or post-hypnotic suggestions in an effective and risk-free way.

Richard Nongard offers another fractionation-based induction that delightfully fits into the pre-talk. Over at howtodoinductions.com, we call Richard's induction (or, at least, our version of it) the Fractionation Conversation.[1]

The Fractionation Conversation demonstrates a useful principle employed by Dave Elman. Building on the work of Hippolyte Bernheim, Elman believed that when you take a person in and out of Hypnosis, they tend to go

---

1 See our take on Nongard's induction at
http://www.howtodoinductions.com/inductions/fractionation

more deeply into trance each time they return.[2]

Nongard offers, as an everyday example, those times when the alarm clock goes off and you hit the snooze button. Just do that two or three times and when you eventually get up you are more tired than when the alarm initially went off. Imagine how deeply you would sleep if someone crept-in and turned the alarm off after you'd hit snooze for the third time![3]

It seems to me that fractionation depends, at least in part, on what Stephen Brooks refers to as "frustrating the trance", or simply delayed gratification. The client is either just about to enter into hypnosis, or is presently enjoying it, when you pull them out of it. This means that when they next sense the opportunity to go back 'in', they do so quickly, eagerly and usually to a greater depth.

This is a useful principle for the hypnotist, making our task so much easier. However, it is especially useful when it comes to experientially teaching someone how to re-enter hypnosis. It means that you can start from any point, without having to achieve 'deep' hypnosis before you begin to make your suggestions for re-induction. Your client will progressively go deeper into their experience, as they learn what is expected of them. It is as if you simply take them by the hand and walk them through what they will later be doing.

---

2 Dave Elman (1977). *Hypnotherapy.* Glendale, CA: Westwood Publishing Co. pp. 101-102.

3 Richard Nongard (2007). *Inductions and Deepeners.* PeachTree Professional Education, Inc. pp. 77-78.

Time-saving

As stated above, my original reason for wanting to discover an effective means of re-induction was to save time. This is a common reason often given for choosing rapid inductions over more progressive or relaxation-based inductions. The idea is that people are paying for your time and want to make the most of it. So, why waste time on the induction, when you could put them quickly into hypnosis and get on with the therapy?

On top of that, I could hardly deny that there was a certain attraction to using rapid inductions. It certainly looks more impressive to spectators!

I had hoped that I could use rapid inductions more confidently if I had previously told the client that they would respond well to them. So, my plan was to get them into hypnosis in the way that I was most comfortable with (which, at the time, would probably have been some variation of a Progressive Muscle Relaxation[4]) and then simply tell them that when I later dropped their arm and yelled "Sleep!" they would drop straight back into hypnosis.

As I grew as a hypnotist, two changes happened in my thinking. Firstly, I discovered that rapid inductions were no more difficult than longer inductions. Secondly, I began to see the real therapeutic value of relaxation, making me less eager to completely give up on progressive inductions.

In fact, my whole concept of inductions changed over time, as you will know if you've read *The Anatomy of Inductions*. I began to see that sometimes rapid

---

4 http://www.howtodoinductions.com/inductions/pmr

inductions were what was needed, whereas at other times a PMR was precisely what the situation called for. It was the client's goal, not time or ego, that became the means by which I chose my inductions.

However, I can not deny that there are still occasions when it may be useful to take someone quickly and definitively into hypnosis. For example, you may only have five minutes left in a session when you decide that you want to take them back into hypnosis. On such occasions it can be helpful to know that when you want to, you can easily lead them back into the deepest experience of hypnosis in a matter of seconds.

Self-Hypnosis

If you use PHRIT with a client - either as an induction or to lay the ground for a later re-induction - then you will save yourself the time of having to teach self-hypnosis.

Instead, you can simply give the post-hypnotic suggestion that they will return to hypnosis whenever they follow the steps that you set-up in your PHRIT. Then, within the comfort of their own home, your clients can re-enact the PHRIT process and experience the same results as achieved in your office.

As well as removing the need to teach self-hypnosis as a separate and unrelated process, as you will find below, PHRIT is flexible enough to be explicitly taught as a means of self-hypnosis from the very beginning.

A Framework for Anchors and post-hypnotic suggestions

As well as being a powerful induction and deepener, PHRIT works well as a framework for anchoring and establishing post-hypnotic suggestions.

In fact, PHRIT provides a simple and effective means of setting-up anchors and post-hypnotic suggestions that both you and your clients will find non-threatening, empowering and easy to grasp.

For this reason, even if you have no intention of using the PHRIT process for inductions or re-inductions, you might still find it to be a valuable addition to your hypnotic toolbox.

EXERCISE

Take some time to consider your current approach to inductions and re-inductions.

• Do you tend to stick to the same familiar inductions? If so, why?

• If not, how do you select which inductions to use?

• Do you approach subsequent inductions in the same way as the initial induction?

Looking at the concept of 'delayed gratification', are there any other ways that you can utilise this, aside from employing fractionation during the induction?

REVISITING HYPNOSIS

The Transcript

You will find a transcript below of an occasion when I have used PHRIT with a client. Please note that this is not offered as a script to be followed, but a description of the induction in action.

For the sake of space, I have omitted any therapeutic stories, or suggestions that were made each time the client went back into hypnosis. These parts are signified by the inclusion of ellipses between paragraphs. However, nothing essential to the induction was taken out of this transcript.

The following transcript records a time when PHRIT was employed on an impromptu basis, without preparation or the use of a pre-written script. Often, I may use another induction - like the Leisure Induction[5], Elman[6] or My Friend John[7] - to get started. Or, I may use nothing else but PHRIT. On this occasion, a simple 'fake induction'[8], framed as an experience of relaxation, was enough to achieve our goal.

---

5   http://www.howtodoinductions.com/inductions/leisure

6   http://www.howtodoinductions.com/inductions/elman

7   http://www.howtodoinductions.com/inductions/mfj

8   http://www.howtodoinductions.com/inductions/fake

Hypnotist: "Okay, all you need to do now is simply get yourself comfortable and if at anyone point you want to shift around and get yourself even more comfortable, you can of course do that.

"What I'm going to invite you to do at the beginning is simply pretend that you're relaxed."

Client: [Laughs] "Okay."

H: "Okay? Pretty easy, right?"

C: [Shuffles around in the chair, getting comfortable] "Sure."

H: "And maybe if you were really relaxed, you would close your eyes..."

C: [Closes their eyes.]

H: "Great. So, you're half way there already. You've got yourself comfortable, you've gently closed your eyes and to carry on, I want you to simply think of a time and place when you are relaxed. And it could be anything right now. Could be a relaxing time when you've been lying on the Beach, could be resting in a beautiful Garden, or walking through the forest... or simply snoozing on the Sofa on a lazy Sunday afternoon."

C: [Facial muscles gradually flatten]

H: "That's it. Nice and easy. Just see what you see, hear what you hear and... feel what you feel... You may even notice that every breath you take ...and every beat of your heart ...and every word that I say enables you to go even deeper into recreating this experience that you're in right now.

"Some people find that their conscious mind chooses to notice the sound of phones in the background, or doors opening, or the soothing sound of the air-conditioner, whilst your subconscious continues to go deeper into that nice comfortable experience. And it all serves to remind you what a natural every-day experience this can be.

"And that means you can enjoy the feeling of just letting go. You don't need to pay attention to how relaxed or heavy your body now feels, or wonder just how far you can go down, [voice slowing down slightly] all you need to do is *relax*...

"Of course, that means different things to different people. To some people it refers to a stilling of the body and a calming of the mind. To others it means a deep inner focus, or a state of creativity or resourcefulness. However your subconscious mind chooses to interpret that, whatever it is you need to experience and how ever deep you continue to go, ...it's all fine."

...

[The PHRIT process begins:]

H: "Now that you've seen how quickly you can relax, in a moment - not yet, but in a moment - we'll have you open your eyes and *at that point* I will invite you to take 4 deep breaths... and as you breathe out the 4th time you can say the word 'relax' in your head as you close your eyes. And you can then bring yourself right back to this place.

[Repeats the steps to be taken once the client opens their eyes:]

"So, in a moment I am going to invite you to take four deep breaths, on the 4th breath out you can say the word 'relax' in your head as you close your eyes. You can then bring yourself right back to this place.

"And you can nod your head to let me know that you understand and accept this idea."

C: [Nods head.]

H: "I'll count from 1-3 and when I reach 3 you can open your eyes and we can carry on talking. 1, 2, 3."

C: [Opens eyes]

H: "How was that? You seemed to be enjoying yourself."

C: "Yeah! Felt surprisingly good."

H: "You enjoyed that. [Said as a statement, not a question.] Great. Okay, so when you're ready, you can take four deep breaths and as you breathe out the 4th time you can say the word 'relax' in your head as you close your eyes and take yourself back into that pleasant experience."

C: [Takes four deep breaths, closing their eyes on the fourth breath.]

H: "That's it...

[The second step in the PHRIT process:]

"...Now that you know just how powerful your mind is, and you know how easily you can return to this deep experience of relaxation, I want you to know that the next time you take 4 deep breaths, you can let those eyes close on the fourth breath as you say the word 'relax' in your head - and you can then allow yourself to come right back to this place.

"So, in a moment, you can take 4 deep breaths and as you breathe out the 4th time, you can say the word 'relax' in your head as you let your eyes close. And you can then allow yourself to come right back to this place.

"Just nod your head to let me know that you understand and accept this idea."

C: [Nods head.]

H: "And I will count from 1-3, and on 3 you can open you eyes... 1, 2, 3."

C: [Opens eyes.]

H: "And when you're ready to return, you can take four deep breaths, ...as you say the word 'relax' in your head, as you allow your eyes to close and go back."

C: [Takes four deep breaths, closing their eyes on the fourth breath.]

...

[The third step in the PHRIT process:]

H: "And now I want you to know that the next time you take 4 deep breaths, saying the word 'relax' in your head on the fourth exhalation, your eyes can close and you can can come right back to this place, if not even deeper.

"The next time you take four deep breaths, saying 'relax' in your head on the fourth breath out, those eyes can close and you'll find yourself coming right back to this place, maybe even deeper.

"Nod your head to let me know that you understand and accept this idea."

C: [Nods head.]

H: "And now, as, I count from 1-3, on 3 you can open your eyes... 1, 2, 3."

C: [Opens eyes]

H: "Now, go ahead and take 4 deep breaths..."

C: [Takes four deep breaths, closing their eyes on the fourth breath.]

...

[The fourth step in the PHRIT process:]

H: "Now I want you to know that the next time you take 4 deep breaths, saying the word 'relax' in your head on the fourth exhalation, your eyes will close and you will come right back to this place, if not even deeper.

"The next time you take 4 deep breaths, saying 'relax' in your head on the fourth breath out, your eyes will close and you'll come right back to this place, if not even deeper.

"Nod your head to let me know that you understand and accept this idea."

C: [Nods head.]

H: "And so as I count from 1-3, on 3 you can open your eyes... 1, 2, 3."

C: [Opens eyes]

H: "Now, go ahead and take 4 deep breaths..."

[As the Client breathes out the fourth time their eyes close and their head drops down. They appear to instantly enter into a deep state of hypnosis.]

EXERCISE

Re-read the previous transcript and take note of anything that you might have done differently.

Visit howtodoinductions.com and read the inductions referenced in the above transcript.

Which of the inductions do you feel best fit with the PHRIT process?

Are there any inductions that you feel would *not* work well with PHRIT?

What reasons might there be for starting with another induction, rather than simply using PHRIT as the sole induction from the beginning?

Finally, re-read the transcript once more and take note of anything that surprises, confuses or intrigues you.

REVISITING HYPNOSIS

Anchors & Post-Hypnotic Suggestions

Before we break down this very simple procedure, it will be beneficial to spend some time looking at the whole area of Anchors and post-hypnotic suggestions.

I have my own theories as to why these things work, but it's more useful for our purposes to focus on the how. I will include my thoughts on the nature of anchoring and post-hypnotic suggestions. However, for our purposes, I would like to focus on the practicalities of working with anchors and post-hypnotic suggestions, as well as seeing how these are experienced by our clients.

Conditioned Connections

The simplest way to think of Anchoring may be to view it as the process of conditioning connections between a stimulus and a desired response. This can happen unintentionally or intentionally (naturally or artificially), so it might be helpful to give an example of each.

Natural Anchoring

I visited Calcutta, India in 1992. It was a life-changing experience; 8 weeks of bombardment on my senses and emotions. As a red-head, I spent every day caked in sunscreen, desperately darting for the cover of shade whenever I could find it.

Later that year, I visited my home-town on the South Coast of England and was surprised to be greeted by an unexpected day of Sunshine. Fortunately, my hosts had plenty of sunscreen and as I began to apply it, a remarkable thing happened. Instantly, I was transported back to the busy, noisy chaotic streets of that city I had grown to love. Please don't underestimate the reality of this experience. I am not saying that the smell of sunscreen merely reminded me of India. It was far more than that.

I could smell the food stalls I used to walk past on the way to catch the Bus to Mother Theresa's *Prem Dan*. I could hear children laughing and the mercilessly incessant beeping of Taxi horns. I had an emotional response of longing and yet contentment, like the yearning for a long-lost love that you were happy to let go. I had a memory, so clear that it bordered on visual hallucination, of the streets we used to walk down to get to the Marketplace. All of this seemed to be experienced instantly and actually took me by surprise. In fact, it was a while before I actually realised the link between the smell of the Sunscreen and the revivification of 8 weeks in that wonderful land of contradiction.

It seems that my time in India was such an emotionally and sensually powerfully one that it created a connection between the unique smell of sunscreen and all that I had experienced there. That connection, I was to learn, had been 'anchored' in my mind.

However, anchors can also be artificially created.

Artificial Anchoring

A common example used by some Hypnotherapists is that of having someone squeeze their hand into a fist whilst they are in a happy or resourceful state. If this is done at the right time, when the 'state' is at or approaching its height of intensity, it is a relatively straightforward thing to anchor the state to the squeezing of the hand. Later, this anchor can be triggered by squeezing the fist, causing the client to re-experience the previously anchored state.

Throughout this book, you will find a number of transcripts that highlight the use of artificial anchoring. However, I would argue that the PHRIT process itself also makes use of natural anchors, unspoken connections that are formed through the deep experience of fractionation, positive reinforcement and re-induction.

Post-Hypnotic Suggestions

Some people get confused by the difference between anchoring and post-hypnotic suggestions. This is understandable, as at times a post-hypnotic suggestion can involve anchoring and an anchor can be a post-hypnotic suggestions. Yet, they are not exactly the same thing, as both can exist without the other.

Anchoring is reminiscent of 'Pavlov's dog'. If you have not heard of this historic and ground-breaking series of experiments, the following may seem to be all but common sense to you.

However, that was not always the case. In the 1920's, the Russian physiologist, Ivan Pavlov experimented with the 'conditioned reflex' of dogs. Pavlov found that when a bell was rung as food was given to a dog, the dog initially salivated when the food was presented. However, in time, the dog came to associate the sound of the bell with the food and would salivate in response to the the bell, with or without the presence of food.

Post-hypnotic Suggestions are simply suggestions which are given during hypnosis for an action or response to take place after the hypnotic experience. This could be a suggestion to trigger an anchor (e.g. "when you see the podium, you will re-experience that state of confidence"), or it may simply be a suggestion that a particular thing will happen at a particular time, or that from now on a particular action will or will not take place.

[For those of us for whom accuracy is important, strictly speaking - in NLP terms - within Anchoring, it is a 'state' that is anchored, not an action. However, post-hypnotic suggestions may be for an action, a feeling or any kind of physical response to occur.]

The relationship between anchors and post-hypnotic suggestions is that they are both, at core, *unconscious learned behaviours.* It is in this sense that PHRIT is an example of both anchoring and post-hypnotic suggestion.

Let's look at how to anchor a state or feeling, before returning to explore this notion of Unconscious Learned Behaviour - and its relationship to re-inductions - in more depth.

EXERCISE

Consider any 'unintentional' anchors that you may have experienced.

- Perhaps the sound of a can of fizzy drink opening makes you feel thirsty?

- Or the buzzing of an insect makes you nervous?

What was it about those experiences that caused such an effective anchor?

How can you use that to your advantage as a hypnotist?

The Practice of Good Anchoring

Anchoring can seem to be an advanced technique, outside of the reach of all but the most experienced hypnotists. However, although the impact of effective anchoring can be highly significant, the practice of good anchoring is in reality a fairly basic affair. Before we move on to demystify the how of anchoring, let's see an example of it in action.

[Client is sat with their eyes open, having just 'resurfaced' from hypnosis.]

Hypnotist: "You can do this bit with your eyes closed or open, whichever you choose. Whichever helps you focus the most easily."

C: [Closes their eyes.]

H: "And what I would like you to do now is simply recall a time when you did feel confident. It can be any time you like, but make it a good one, you feel really confident...

"You know, that good kinda confidence that

grow inside you. And you can feel it..."

C: [Breaths in and a slight smile appears to form on their lips]

H: "...that's it, a time you can feel right now. And the more that comes back to you, the more you see those sights and hear those sounds, the more you can feel that confidence. Isn't it funny how those feelings can come flooding back now?"

C: [Breaks into a full smile and nods]

H: "And what you can do now, as that confidence grows and grows and spreads and spreads, when you feel that you can barely feel any more confident, I want you to squeeze together the forefinger and thumb on your right hand, to make like an "OK" sign.

"That's it, as if you're locking in that confidence. And as you do that, maybe it increases even more...until you let it go and the confidence can temporarily subside.

"And now, just open your eyes for me. So, tell me, can you remember the first time you successfully tied your shoelaces on your own?"

[Client proceeds to tell a brief story, with questions from me about insignificant data such as the colour of his parent's Car at that point in his life. Essentially, this was a meaningless diversion to break state, whilst simultaneously evoking a memory of success.]

H: "Now, why don't you make that okay sign for me and tell me how good that feels?"

C: "Ha! Yeah, that's good. Yeah!"

H: "Good, huh? Well, this is even better..."

[We then proceeded to go to a future scenario that would previously have made the client nervous. As they reached the first stage where they would usually prepare to feel anxious (which we had previously discussed) they made the okay sign and experienced their body - and indeed their whole experience - being filled with confidence.]

EXERCISE

If you have a willing practice-partner, you might want to begin practising the art of intentional Anchoring.

To start with, simply practice eliciting a simple positive state, such as confidence. You can use Appendix A as a guide here.

When you feel that you have a grasp on eliciting states, move on to anchoring those states.

Alternatively, practice anchoring a positive state on yourself, using the previous transcript as a model to guide you.

The Steps to Good Anchoring

During my time in India, I was not aware that I was creating an association between the smell of sunscreen and the memory of my time there. Yet, it just so happens that the sense of smell is the one most closely connected to memory. That, plus the intensity of everything I experienced - tastes, sights, sounds, heat, emotion - meant that I went through 8 weeks of connecting the two.

Now, when anchoring in the context of hypnosis we do not typically have 8 weeks. Sometimes, we're lucky if we have 8 minutes. Yet, even with such limitations, it is possible to condition a connection so powerful that it releases a flood of positive emotions and well-being.

In fact, the process of anchoring a state is remarkably simple when you know how. Let's first of all look at some of the elements that created my natural and unintentional Indian anchor.

The intensity of the experience

I was only a young man when I travelled to the Sub-continent and I had not been on many other overseas trips. To me, everything about India, and in particular Calcutta, was intense. It was intense both in terms of my physical senses and also in terms of the emotional reactions it provoked in me.

The uniqueness and appropriateness of the stimuli

Sunscreen naturally connects to warmer temperatures, making it perfect for this purpose.

Additionally, it is the olfactory bulb which transmits smell information from the nose to the brain. The olfactory bulb is part of the brain's limbic system, as are the hippocampus and amygdala, which are responsible for generating both emotions and memory. It's no wonder then that the distinct smell of sunscreen triggered my vivid memory.

The repetition of the stimulus

My most sacred ritual when in India was the daily application of sunscreen. In fact, it would be repeated throughout the day, every day. Of course, it would also later be replicated when I would go to apply sunscreen on a sunny day at some later date.

It is interesting how closely these points mirror the keys to good Anchoring often recommended by NLP Trainers:

1) Intensity

The intensity of the experience affects how easily, quickly and strongly you can anchor the connection. Think of how a phobic response can be learned (or, anchored) after just one emotionally intense experience. Conversely, if an experience is less intense, it can take longer - or more repetitions - to create a strong association.

2) Timing

There are debates as to the most effective time to anchor an association. Many NLP trainers and practitioners will say that it is important to do so at the peak of the experience. However, I am with Robert Dilts in suggesting that the most effective time to anchor is just before the peak is reached.

As the intensity of the experience lessens, so does the association. If you can maintain this intensity for a longer period of time it is more likely the anchor will be established.

3) Uniqueness

Anchoring is most effective when it involves an anchor that is uniquely associated to the experience. This saves confusion or watering-down the connection. As I suggested above, I also prefer to find a trigger that is particularly appropriate to the desired response, e.g. making a diver's "OK" sign with my finger and thumb if I am anchoring a state of confidence, a clenched fist for strength and so on.

4) Repetition

The more you repeat the process of anchoring a

response to a stimuli, the more likely you are to be successful. Additionally, it naturally follows that the anchor needs to be something that can be replicated at a later time. So, don't anchor sitting in the chair in your treatment room with a state of Focus, if you want them to be able to replicate that out in the real world.

Anchoring Representational Systems

Anchoring can take place with any of the sensory modalities. That is, you can anchor sights, sounds, feelings, smells or tastes. An example of Anchoring that utilises more than one representational system is the Visual Squash.[9]

Break State

After you have established an anchor, it is good practice to 'break state' before continuing. This is simply a temporary distraction or separation to move them out of the state you have just anchored. Unless you break state between establishing an anchor and testing it, you will have no real way of knowing if it has actually worked. You would effectively have them test the anchor to revisit a state that they have not yet fully left.

To break state, you can simply ask an irrelevant question, make an illogical statement, or have them carry out an action such as jumping up and down, shaking their body or getting up to get a glass of water.

---

9 Jess Marion, (2015). *The Visual Squash: An NLP Tool for Radical Change.* New York: Changing Minds.

As well as being an essential aspect of anchoring, breaking state can be a useful therapeutic tool. A relatively inconspicuous example of this is the opening question I employ with my clients. Simply due to the fact that they are visiting a therapist, they often enter my office in a Problem frame of mind. My chosen preference is to work with them in a Solution or Possibilities mindset. So, to break the connection between being in my office and dwelling on their problems, I often begin with a seemingly irrelevant question the minute they walk through the door.

"Tell me, what's your favourite comedy?"

"What's the last cartoon you can remember watching?"

"Who is your favourite comedian?"

As well as moving them to a more enjoyable state, questions such as this break the link between being in my office and feeling overwhelmed, focusing on problems or taking the role of a victim. Instead, I take whatever answer they provide and link it to one of a number of cheesy jokes that I have in reserve.

When they politely laugh, I say something like, "The worrying thing is, this is my day job!" which functions as a nice bit of mind-reading and leads to my next question:

"What about you? What do you do when you're not listening to bad therapy jokes?"

I follow that up with a question about how they spend their free-time and we are then a nice distance removed from their problem. We are also in a good position to access a resourceful frame of mind by discussing their strengths and things they do well. The seemingly irrelevant opening question functioned both to break state and set a new direction for us to proceed.

However, breaking state does not need to be so involved. It really can be as simple as asking them what the colour of their front door is, asking them to change seats or telling them the name of your first school teacher and asking theirs. Sure, you may get some strange looks, but in my experience, people tend to presume it's all part of the therapy and can be very forgiving of such quirks.

EXERCISE

Consider the difference – if any – between a pattern-interrupt and breaking state.

[A pattern-interrupt is the intentional breaking of a habitual or automatic pattern of thought or behaviour.]

Continue to practice anchoring. However, this time practice both with and without breaking state. Notice the difference in effect.

Are there times that you might want to intentionally *not* break state?

REVISITING HYPNOSIS

Unconscious Learned Behaviours

I stated above that post-hypnotic suggestions and anchoring both involve *unconscious learned behaviours*. It may be obvious that this is the case with anchoring. After all, it is rather clearly a process of conditioning. Yet, how is that the case with post-hypnotic suggestions, which may only be given once?

Let me try to explain my position from the perspective of a client experiencing such procedures. I may give the suggestion that when someone emerges from hypnosis, they will no longer be able to remember the number between 3 and 5. I bring them up and ask them to count the fingers on my hands and they count to 11, because they jumped to the number 5 when they reached my 4th finger.

Similarly, I might suggest that someone laughs when they see a red Pen or feels calm curiosity when they see a Spider.

It may seem that when such actions are later carried out they happen automatically, completely outside of the agency of the client. Yet, there is a host of research to suggest precisely the opposite. It would seem that when someone, for example, misses out the number 4, there is invariably part of them that is intentionally restraining the information from being recalled. They may or may not be completely aware of it, but both anecdotal evidence and scientific research appear to demonstrate that the seemingly 'automatic' behaviour happens because the client intends to do it.[10]

I would actually argue that this is not simply the case with hypnotic phenomena, but is also true with something like a spider phobia. If that does not yet sound particularly plausible, just think of the old phobic response as an anchored behaviour which through hypnosis is replaced with a new and alternative outcome. The client may not feel like they are intentionally choosing the new behaviour, yet they are actively doing different things to that which they did when they 'did' their phobia. They are simply doing so outside of their conscious awareness or attention.

In all of these cases, the client has learned how to respond. This is precisely why effective post-hypnotic suggestions are always couched in terms that the client can understand. They need to be able to do what they are asked to do and that requires them knowing what is expected of them.

[I am avoiding academic scientific discussion as much as possible, but if you would like to read some more along these lines, I would recommend familiarising yourself with some of the Recommended Reading at the end of the book.]

Not only does the client learn how to respond, but through things like future pacing, they can learn when to respond. The only difference between these responses feeling hypnotic and them feeling intentional is whether

10 Cf. http://www.mheap.com/nature%20of%20hypnosis.html, as well as sources cited in the bibliography.

or not the client is aware of deliberately intending to do them.

You may already have made the connection between this point and the psycho-educational theory of the *Four Stages of Competence*:

Unconscious incompetence

When operating at the stage of *Unconscious Incompetence*, the individual involved does not understand or know how to do something. Additionally, they do not necessarily recognize the deficit. They may deny the usefulness of the skill, or simply be unaware that they lack it. It is necessary that such an individual acknowledges their own incompetence, and the value of the new skill, before moving on to the next stage.

Conscious incompetence

The next stage, *Conscious Incompetence*, is the point at which although the individual does not understand or know how to do something, they do recognise their deficit, as well as the value of a new skill.

Conscious competence

Conscious Competence is when an individual understands or knows how to do something. However, demonstrating the skill or knowledge requires concentration, often intensely. There is a heavy and deliberate conscious involvement in executing the new skill.

Unconscious competence

At the stage of *Unconscious Competence*, the individual has had so much practice with a skill that it has become "second nature" and can be performed easily. As a result, the skill can be performed while executing another task. The individual is able to carry out the skill with little deliberate thought or attention. They are also able to teach it to others.

So, it is seen that there are actions we carry out without being consciously aware that we are the ones doing so (e.g. Driving whilst experiencing the frequently mentioned 'highway hypnosis'.) This may be for any number of reasons. It could be that such actions do not require conscious thought because they are perceived to be simple and make use of natural processes. It might be because trauma or overwhelming emotional reactions have taught us not to consciously dwell on them. Or it may be that they have been learned to such a degree that they are second nature.

Post-hypnotic suggestions, I would argue, rely on this very phenomenon. Instead of giving instructions that are automatically carried out, we as hypnotists make suggestions that the client understands, agrees to accept and intends to carry out. They may just not be aware of that.

Conditioned Connections, Post-Hypnotic Suggestions and Re-inductions?

You could be forgiven for wondering what this all has to do with re-inductions! So, let me get straight to the point. It is my contention that the most effective way to carry out a re-induction is as an anchored post-hypnotic suggestion.

[Additionally, I would suggest that a well-rounded approach to re-inductions - such as that found in PHRIT - teaches both hypnotists and their clients an effective process for anchoring and post-hypnotic suggestions.]

It is certainly possible to carry out a re-induction that is not an anchored response. For example, the following will often suffice:

Hypnotist: "Remember how nice you said it felt after our session last week? Well, what I'd like you to do now is just take a nice deep breath...hold it for a moment... And as you breath out, you can close your eyes and go back down inside... Right back to that nice special place..."

However, for all of the reasons I mentioned towards the beginning of this book, I now prefer to use the progressive learning exercise that we call PHRIT.

The non-anchored re-induction fails to recognise that

some people will not yet have learned how to return to "that nice special place". They may well enjoy the experience of being there, but that does not mean they know (consciously or non-consciously) how to return simply by closing their eyes.

Such a practice is asking the client to do something that they had presumed was your doing. Even if they know how to, for example, relax themselves, that doesn't mean they know how to do so without 30 minutes of muscle relaxation or a nice warm bath.

To use the language of the Four Stages of Competence, it is as if you are asking them to employ unconscious competence, when they have not yet even reached the level of conscious mediocrity.

Why not simply take the time to condition a connection between exhaling / closing their eyes and relaxing? And then give a post-hypnotic suggestion for experiencing that relaxation and returning to hypnosis. Finally, intensify all of that through fractionation and repeat the process.

Help your clients learn all of this gradually and experientially and you are far more likely to achieve the results you are after.

EXERCISE

Set aside some time to look into the works recommended at the end of this book. In particular, you may want visit the theories of Andrew Salter or Alfred Barrios.

Salter taught that 'Hypnosis is nothing but an aspect of conditioning.'

Do you agree? If so, why? If not, why not?

If you disagree, in what ways are you still able to use the idea of conditioned connections in your hypnotic practice?

How do you feel about the idea that the creation and removal of a Spider Phobia are both examples of 'conditioned connections'?

Think of any specific and practical ways that you could incorporate a fresh appreciation for conditioning in your hypnotic practice.

REVISITING HYPNOSIS

GRAHAM OLD

Collapsing Anchors

Collapsing an anchor is a process that allows us to neutralise the power of negative anchors. As mentioned previously, an anchor may be created naturally or artificially. If an unwanted anchor is resulting in an undesirable state, then the technique known as collapsing anchors can be employed to break the association.

To collapse an anchor, we first identify the problem state, so that we know which alternative positive state is desired. The purpose is not to dwell on the past, but to give direction to a positive future.

Having described what they want from a positive anchor, the client is invited to recall having felt that way and the positive anchor is installed in the usual way.

A Break State is then employed and after the client has 'come down', the anchor is tested.

The negative anchor is then established. Preferably this will be the opposite of the positive, so e.g. involving the left hand instead of the right.

After breaking state again, each state can be fired in turn, without breaking state between them. This is a powerful convincer to the client, as they experience themselves switching between the two.

Finally fire both anchors at once... this will cause a

little confusion while your physiology attempts to achieve both states simultaneously, now break the negative state but keep the positive state going.

To test the success of the collapse break state and fire the negative anchor, the result should be a neutral state, somewhere between the two states. If the negative state persists positive anchors can be stacked on the same anchor and the procedure repeated.

It is important to create a very powerful positive state, even if this requires stacking states together, as the positive state must be stronger than the negative state to collapse the negative anchors for example, we ask a client to imagine a positive experience then touch their arm or hand as that experience reaches a peak of intensity.

The following transcript demonstrates this simple yet powerful process in action:

Hypnotist: "I wonder if we've got time to squeeze one more bit of goodness in? Lot's of people find this useful, so I'd like to let you experience it."

Client: "Okay."

H: "In a moment, I'll have you close your eyes, so that you can really go into this experience, but before you do that, let me just explain what is going to happen.

"I am going to have you put both of your

hands flat on your knees and what we are going to do is have you recall a time when you felt the complete opposite to how you felt in that interview. That could be whatever you choose: happy, confident, beautiful, adventurous - it's up to you. And when you are feeling that as much as you possibly can, I will ask you to say, "Now" and I will touch you on the back of one of your hands - and you can choose which hand - and then we'll just have you open your eyes.

"Happy with that?"

C: "Yeah, definitely."

H: "Okay, so we've talked a little bit about how you feel during Job Interviews - and in particular during those two job interviews we've called 'Water' and 'July'. And I think the word you used was that those interviews still 'haunt' you. Is that right?"

C: "Yeah. Like I can't shake it, the feeling."

H: "And we saw that quite vividly when discussing a future interview and you got quite tearful."

C: "Yeah."

H: "So, how would you have wanted to have

felt during those interviews?

"In fact, let me put it a bit stronger, what feeling or emotion or state of mind could be so powerful that even if the interviews went the way they did, you could still be left feeling great?"

C: [Thinks for a while...] "I'd have to say, 'Invincible'."

 H: "Ooh, invincible. That's a good one. Okay, and what hand would you like to associate with that invincible feeling?"

C: [Lifts her right fingers up.]

H: "Okay, your right hand. Well, now then, I would like you to think of a time when you have felt invincible. So, to really get into this, go ahead and close your eyes."

C: [Closes her eyes and shuffles in the chair.]

H: "...And get comfortable and just think of a time when you have felt invincible. I mean, REALLY invincible. Make it a happy memory or experience; some time that you just felt unbeatable, on top of the world, invincible. This could be something from the last couple of days, or the last few weeks, the last few years or from any point in your life.

"You can do anything. There's nothing you cannot conquer. You are invincible!"

C: [Smiles.]

H: "You've got one."

C: "Yeah."

H: "Okay, well, now I want you to focus on that. And, in fact, you can just go ahead and step into that scene, step into your body and see what you saw, hear what you heard and feel what you felt. You can even make it bigger and brighter and just feel that feeling more and more intensely. At the point that you are feeling that "invincible" the strongest you can just nod your head to let me know."

C: [After a brief pause, the client smiles and nods their head.]

H: "And you can let your whole body enjoy that feeling of invincibility now... That's it, from the tip of your head, to that growing smile on your face, to your shoulders and all the way down to the tip of your toes."

C: [Their smile broadens and they nod their head 2-3 times vigorously.]

H: [Leans over and clearly touches their right hand, just above the middle knuckle for a couple of seconds.]

H: "Okay, you can open your eyes. So, what was your first school teacher called?"

C: "Um, Miss Turner, I think."

H: "Did you like her?"

C: "Yeah. She was strict, but I tended to be a bit of a Teacher's Pet, so I quite liked her."

H: "My first teacher was Mrs. Dale. My memory of her is that she had no patience whatsoever, but I guess the reality is that we drove her to the edge every day and she was probably a saint not to lose it more often!"

C: [Laughs]

H: "Okay, so, now just put your hand back on your knee. And tell me what happens when I Touch it here?" [Touches the back of their right hand, just above the middle knuckle.]

H: "Or now? Or now?" [Firing the anchor each time.]

C: [Smiles] "Cor!"

H: "Isn't it great to know that whenever you want to feel invincible again you can simply touch yourself on this knuckle and instantly feel this feeling?"

C: "Yeah. That's amazing."

H: "Well, would you like to do something even more amazing?"

C: "Ok."

H: "I should warn you before we begin that this involves us very briefly bringing back some of the feelings connected to 'Water' and 'July'. It'll only be for a few moments, but it will be less comfortable than what we've just done.

"However, I can tell you that afterwards you will feel great. So, do you want to see just how powerful your invincible mind can be?"

C: "Sure"

H: "Great.

"So, you can put both hands back on your knees and close your eyes. Now I want you to revisit one of those previous job interviews, or a similar experience or memory that left you feeling the same way. Okay?"

REVISITING HYPNOSIS

C: [Nods]

H: "Okay, so now you can go ahead and step into your body and see what you saw, hear what you heard, and feel, really feel what you felt. And when you are feeling that as strongly as you can, I want you to nod your head."

C: [Frowns slightly and then nods.] "Okay."

H: [Leans over and touches their left hand, just above the middle knuckle for a couple of seconds.]

"Okay, you can open your eyes... and I want you to know that... you don't have to feel like that, you can always feel like this.

[As I said "You can always feel like this," I then touched their middle knuckle on their right hand.]

"Whenever you feel like this [touches left hand] You can always feel like this... [touches right hand]

"Isn't that amazing?"

C: "Yeah. [Laughs.] That's cool."

H: "Now, do you want to see something even more cool? It's a little weird and possibly even confusing, but it will only take around ten seconds and afterwards you will be totally blown-away. So, do you want to see this final step?"

C: "Okay, yeah."

H: "So, put both hands back on your knees and look at me."

[Fires both anchors at the same time and holds on for 5 seconds. Then removes the negative anchor. Waits 5 seconds and removes the positive anchor.]

H: "That's a bit weird, isn't it?"

C: [Blinks.] "Yeah. Kinda cool though."

H: "So, what happens when I touch here now?" [Touches left hand.]

C: "Er... It's gone. Wow, it's like the feeling's dead."

H: "And if you think of 'July' or 'Water', what does that feel like now?"

C: "Nothing. It's, just, like, numb."

H: "Okay, well try just one last thing for me here. I want you to go to the future and think of a job interview that you're going to have."

C: "Ok."

H: "And how does that feel?"

C: "It's like there's nothing there."

H: "So, what happens - whilst you're there - if you touch here..." [Touches back of right hand]

C: "Yes! Ha, I feel excellent. Like I know I'm gonna ace it."

H: "Invincible?"

C: "Definitely!"

The Basic Process

After such a meandering discussion, let's remind ourselves of the basic PHRIT process.

To begin, induce Hypnosis, or even just enable the client to relax. Then:

1) Tell the client that when they take 4 deep breaths, as they breathe out the 4th time, they can *bring themselves back* into the experience they are currently having. Get their agreement.

Have them open their eyes, remind them of what to do and then *invite them to do it*. They bring themselves back.

2) Tell the client that when they next take 4 deep breaths, as they breathe out the 4th time they can *allow themselves to come back* into the experience they are currently having.

Have them open their eyes, remind them of what to do and then have them do it. *They allow themselves to come back.*

3) Tell them that when they next breathe out the 4th time they can *find themselves coming back* into the experience they are currently having.

Have them open their eyes, and tell them to take 4 deep breaths. T*hey find themselves going back.*

4) Finally, tell them that when they next breathe out the 4th time they *will* go straight back...

Have them open their eyes. Tell them to take 4 deep breaths. *They go straight back.*

EXERCISE

Practice using the PHRIT process with a practice-partner.

Notice the parts of the process that work particularly well for you.

Be aware of any parts that you or your practice-partner appear to struggle with.

Experiment with the process and begin to take note of ways that you might want to adapt or develop it.

Does the process fit naturally with your current style or approach?

Are there adaptations you could make so that PHRIT better serves you and your clients needs?

Perhaps there are parts of PHRIT which challenge your current style or approach, or which you want to give more thought to.

REVISITING HYPNOSIS

Breaking it Down

The transcript of PHRIT in action above - plus the consequent discussion of anchoring and post-hypnotic suggestions - may all seem a bit long-winded. They may even make this induction seem convoluted and overly complex. It is not. As you practice and grow familiar with it, I am sure that you will find it to be wonderfully simple and yet surprisingly powerful and flexible.

The key to PHRIT is *progressive permissive fractionation*. That is, the progression from permissive to direct suggestions, accompanied by powerful fractionation.

Permissive --> Direct

Clients may have seen Stage Hypnotists and others seemingly controlling their subjects, with shouts of "Sleep!" Yet, if your clients are anything like mine, for many of them, the last thing they want to feel is that you can take them into and out of hypnosis at your command.

However, I have not yet had anyone object to being taught how to do this for themselves. So, we begin with teaching them how to take themselves back into hypnosis. Once they have found that they can do this easily enough - and even enjoy the experience -

something very significant has happened:

- They have begun to trust you and let their guard down
- They have begun to believe they can do what you ask of them

The language used is permissive, inviting and empowering. At least, it starts off that way. The suggestion is made and agreement is sought. The client is then brought back and taken "under" once again. The suggestion is then made again, only slightly less permissively.

This process of making increasingly direct suggestions continues until the re-induction is accepted - *and experienced* - as an automatic reaction to a direct and straightforward instruction.

Another way to view this, perhaps more in line with the experience of the client, is that they gradually move from intentional responses through to unconscious learned behaviour.

Progressive Fractionation

In addition to teaching the client how to progressively accept your suggestions, the repeated experience of being taken in and out of hypnosis usually results in the client going "deeper" each time. This is due to the fractionation or 'frustrating the trance' that we spoke of earlier.

More often than not, the client experiences this as confirmation that the process is working, as they find the hypnosis intensifying with each journey back. Therefore, the words 'or even more deeply' seen in some of the transcripts take on special significance. My reason for including them is not because I believe they work in and of themselves. Instead, I use them as an exercise in pacing and leading. My suspicion is that the client will naturally experience the process as one of going back into hypnosis more quickly and deeply each time. When that happens, they will associate it with my earlier suggestion and receive further evidence that i) this is working and ii) they can trust and follow my suggestions.

An additional benefit of this experience of intensification, is that it is possible to start the PHRIT process with only a light level of relaxation.

Rewarding Repetition

You will remember from above that an important element in setting up an anchor is the use of repetition. This is evident in PHRIT, both in the fractionation and the instruction that is given throughout:

"...the next time you take 4 deep breaths
...eyes close on the fourth breath
...say the word "relax" in your head
...back to this place."

Additionally, as an outcome of the fractionation involved, PHRIT is experienced as an enjoyable and rewarding process. After all, nothing beats the nice taste of delayed gratification.

From the days of Pavlov himself, we have known that

positive reinforcement was a considerable ally in establishing conditioned connections. This is clearly demonstrable in the readiness and ease with which people respond to the PHRIT process.

An Anchored Response

The preceding discussion may have made left you more than aware of the final, almost imperceptible, aspect of the PHRIT induction.

As well as taking your clients through a process of increasingly direct suggestions, the PHRIT process - as seen in the transcript above - anchors a connection between saying the word "relax" in their head, exhaling, their eyes closing and then returning to hypnosis. This may seem like a natural and automatic part of the induction, but that does not mean it is not vitally important.

The uniqueness and appropriateness of anchors has been mentioned previously. So, for example we may anchor confidence with an "OK" symbol, strength with a fist and relaxation or "sleep" with the closing of our eyes. Although hypnosis is not a state of sleep - or relaxation, for that matter - our clients are not usually as concerned with such distinctions as we are.

Through experiencing a deepening fractionation, connected with i) thinking the word "relax, ii) closing their eyes and iii) exhaling - all experienced as one action - your client will have anchored a deep experience of hypnosis with the simple act of closing their eyes as outlined within the PHRIT process. This ensures that when they later close their eyes - or whatever you have anchored - the whole process is accessed via that simple action.

EXERCISE

Continue to practice with the PHRIT process.

Which of the 4 aspects do you find most valuable:

1. Progression from indirect to direct suggestions

2. Fractionation

3. Reward

4. Anchoring

Are there ways that you can apply these 4 aspects into your other inductions?

Can these 4 aspects be incorporated into your wider practice of hypnosis and hypnotherapy?

Variations & Applications

Once you have grasped the concept of PHRIT, there are countless alternative routes you could take with it. I will mention just a few.

The One-breath trigger

It is possible to add a variation to PHRIT, where one less breath is taken on each re-induction. This can culminate in the re-induction being triggered with a simple breath, or the word "relax", or a tap on the knee (or whatever trigger you anchor).

This variation is employed as follows:

- Tell the client that when they take 4 deep breaths, as they breathe out the 4th time, [Optional: and say the work "relax" in their head] they can bring themselves back into the experience they are currently having.

- Tell the client that as they take *3* deep breaths, as they breathe out the *3rd* time [Optional: and say the work "relax" in their head] they can allow themselves to come back into the experience they are currently having.

- Tell them that when they next breathe out the *2nd* time [Optional: and say the work "relax" in their head] they can find themselves coming back into the experience they are currently having.

- Finally, tell them that when they next breathe out [Optional: and say the work "relax" in their head] they will go straight back...

Self-hypnosis

The transcript of PHRIT in action provided in part 1 is a perfect example of how the process can be used as a self-hypnosis protocol. In fact, all that would need to be added to that example would be a brief introductory explanation:

Hypnotist: "I am now going to teach you a process, which you can repeat at home, to rapidly take yourself to a place of inner focus, calm and resourcefulness..."

And then move straight into PHRIT, as usual.

As an induction in its own right

It is possible to move straight into the PHRIT process without any other induction. The following transcript involves a client who had an interest in Stage Hypnosis and acts like Derren Brown. (They had been one of the subjects in a Stage Hypnosis show). They considered themselves knowledgeable in what we might term pop psychology and the hypnotist employed their terminology in a number of places.[11] When asked how they expected therapeutic hypnosis to differ to Stage Hypnosis, they said, "I guess it would be a similar experience, but less 'showy'? So, I'm expecting the same effect on my end, but more clinical techniques from your end. Maybe gentler?"

> Hypnotist: "Well, to start off, you can get yourself comfortable and maybe you want to go ahead and close your eyes... And, yeah, you can shuffle around, getting yourself nice and comfortable, in <u>body and mind</u>.
>
> "And perhaps you can think of a time when you have felt similar to that <u>dream-state</u> you so enjoyed. An occasion when your mind <u>floats</u> while your <u>body rests</u>. Or maybe you recall that previous experience of hypnosis itself. Any time when your mind has felt <u>free</u> as your body just <u>sleeps</u>.
>
> "And in a moment - not yet, but in a moment - we'll have you open your eyes and then I will invite you to take 4 deep breaths... and as you breathe out the 4th time you can say the word '<u>Sleep</u>' in your head as you close your eyes.

---

11 Examples of the client's terminology are seen in the underlined words in this transcript.

And you can then take yourself off to that dream-land, that place of peace and calm - where your conscious mind drifts off, leaving me free to speak to your subconscious.

H: "Okay, so you can can ahead and open your eyes..."

Client: [Opens eyes, raises eyebrows and smiles]

H: "And just take four deep breaths now... that's it... and as you breathe out the 4th time, you say the word 'Sleep' in your head and close your eyes. You can then take yourself right back to that pleasant place..."

C: [Takes four deep breaths, closing their eyes on the fourth breath.]

H: "That's it...

"...And now that you know how easily you can take yourself back to that deep experience of trance, I want you to know that the next time you take 4 deep breaths, you can let those eyes close on the fourth breath as you say the word 'Sleep' in your head - and you can then allow yourself to come right back to this place.

"So, in a moment, you can take 4 deep breaths

and as you breathe out the 4th time, you can say the word 'Sleep' in your head. And you can then allow yourself to come right back to this place.

"Just nod your head to let me know that you understand and accept this idea."

C: [Nods head.]

H: "And I will count from 1-3, and on 3 you can open you eyes... 1, 2, 3."

C: [Opens eyes.]

H: "How was that?"

C: "Wonderful! I feel like I've had a power-nap already!" [Laughs]

H: "Great! Well, when you're ready to return, you can take four deep breaths, ...and as you say the word 'Sleep' in your head, you let those eyes close and allow yourself to go back."

C: [Takes four deep breaths, closing their eyes on the fourth breath.]

H: "That's it... Going back to that place you know so well. Enjoy that.

"And the next time you take 4 deep breaths, saying the word 'Sleep' in your head on the fourth exhalation, your eyes can close and you'll find yourself coming right back to this place, if not even deeper.

"The next time you take four deep breaths, saying 'Sleep' in your head on the fourth breath out, those eyes can close and you'll come right back to this place, maybe even deeper.

"Nod your head to let me know that you understand and accept this idea."

C: [Nods head.]

H: "And now, as, I count from 1-3, on 3 you can open your eyes... 1, 2, 3."

C: [Opens eyes]

H: "Now, go ahead and take 4 deep breaths..."

C: [Takes four deep breaths, closing their eyes on the fourth breath.]

H: "Now I want you to know that the next time you take 4 deep breaths, saying the word 'Sleep' in your head on the fourth exhalation, your eyes will close and you will come right back to this place, if not even deeper.

"The next time you take 4 deep breaths, saying 'Sleep' in your head on the fourth breath out, your eyes will close and you'll come right back to this place, if not even deeper.

"Nod your head to let me know that you understand and accept this idea."

C: [Nods head.]

H: "And so as I count from 1-3, on 3 you can open your eyes... 1, 2, 3."

C: [Opens eyes]

H: "Now, go ahead and take 4 deep breaths..."

As a process for Post-Hypnotic Suggestions

Whenever I intend to set a post-hypnotic suggestion, I now always precede it with a suggestion for re-induction. That way, the client knows that they can do this and does not doubt or question the effectiveness of the suggestions.

Once PHRIT has worked, I find that all other post-hypnotic suggestions (all expressed in a similar progressive or repetitive way) are accepted much more easily.

For example, if you wanted to set an anchor that a client would feel confident whenever she made an "OK" sign with her forefinger and thumb, you might take the example provided in 'The Practice of Good Anchoring' and apply the PHRIT process:

> "And what you can do now, as that confidence grows and grows and spreads and spreads, when you feel that you can hardly contain any more confidence, I want you to squeeze together the forefinger and thumb on your right hand, to make like an OK sign.

> "That's it, as if you're locking in that confidence. And as you do that, maybe it increases even more...until you let it go and the confidence can temporarily subside."

Now...

1) Tell the client that when they next make an "OK" sign they can recall and revive and re-experience that surge of confidence.

Get their agreement.

Remind them of what to do and then invite them to do it. They take themselves back into the experience of confidence.

2) Tell the client that when they next make an "OK" sign they can allow themselves to go back into the confidence they have just experienced.

Remind them of what to do and then have them do it. They allow themselves to go back.

3) Tell them that when they next make an "OK" sign, they can find themselves going back into the confidence they have been experiencing.

Remind them of what to do and then have them do it. They find themselves going back.

4) Finally, tell them that when they next make an "OK" sign, they will experience a surge of confidence.

Remind them of what to do and then have them do it.. They go straight back.

This is simply an example, but I'm sure you get the idea. You use the PHRIT process to teach and rehearse the steps of good anchoring and post-hypnotic suggestions.

A Fuller Anchoring Process

In fact, we can employ PHRIT to provide a much fuller experience of anchoring. We do this by suggestion and by utilising the built-in repetition to intensify the experience.

The following example demonstrates this well. This was an occasion where a client described feeling "powerless" at work, despite being successful both at work and in their private life. One of the ways we addressed this was by setting a trigger for a feeling of "confident control" that they could fire whenever they wanted to access that state.

Hypnotist: "And what I would like you to do now is simply recall one of the many times when you do feel that experience of strong confident control. Just go ahead and locate one and let me know when you're there."

Client: [Nods their head.] "Got it."

H: "You've got it. Good. Now *really* get it. I want you to *experience that right now*. As much as you possibly can. That familiar feeling spreading in your bones, in your muscles... that's it... filling you up now.

"And as you *feel that*, notice what you looked like when you are in control. Maybe you notice that you stand differently, or perhaps you smile differently. I don't know. Go ahead and see for yourself. And as you notice that, maybe you've already become aware how it feels when you look that way. So, now go ahead and step into that image and see through those confident controlled eyes. I wonder how different things look to you when you are in control.

"Just see what you see, hear what you hear and feel what you feel.

[A rather clichéd phrase, but it helps the client re-create a fuller experience by focusing through 3 different modalities.]

"And as that reaches its peak, what you can do is go ahead and squeeze your right fist together. Almost as if you're locking in that experience, grabbing hold of it and keeping it in there."

C: [Clenches their fist and squeezes.]

H: "That's it. And as you do that, maybe it increases even more...until you let it go and that feeling can temporarily subside."

[This anchoring is repeated with 3 other experiences. We then *break state* and continue with the 1st stage of the PHRIT process:]

H: "Now, in a moment - not yet, but in a moment - I want you to clench that fist again and recall and revive and re-experience that surge of confident control. Just nod your head if you understand and agree."

C: [Nods their head.]

H: "Okay, so just go ahead and clench your fist and take yourself back to that experience of strength and confident control."

C: [Clenches their fist and visibly expands their chest out.]

H: "Now you can let go and that feeling subsides."

[We move on to stage 2 of the PHRIT process:]

H: "And in a moment I want you to clench that fist again and as you do so, you can allow yourself to go back into that confident control. And maybe as you're practising this it gets more powerful with each repetition.

"Nod your head if you understand and agree."

C: [Nods their head.]

H: "Okay, so just go ahead and clench your fist and allow yourself to go back to that confident control... and even more."

C: [Squeezes fist and smiles.]

H: "That's it. And I wonder if it does get more powerful each time, maybe your subconscious bringing in other experiences of confidence without you even knowing... finding that your confidence increases and increases each time you do this.

"And now you can let go..."

[Stage 3 of the PHRIT process:]

H: "In a moment I'll ask you to clench your fist and as you do so you'll find yourself going back into that confidence and even more. Increasing with every visit. Nod your head to let me know that you understand and agree."

C: [Nods their head.]

H: "So go ahead and clench your fist and find yourself going back to that confident control."

C: [Squeezes their fist.]

H: "That's it. More and more confident...

"And now you can let go..."

[Stage 4:]

H: "Now, the next time you squeeze that fist together you will automatically experience a surge of confident control. More and more strength and confidence, naturally filling you from head to toe. Nod your head to let me know that you understand and agree."

C: [Nods their head.]

H: "So go ahead and clench your fist and..."

C: [Clenches their fist and visibly expands their chest out.]

H: "That's it... immediately experiencing that confident control."

[We then broke state again and took the client to a future scenario when they were struggling to feel confident. They fired the anchor and experienced and sudden and powerful rush of confidence.]

Used in this way, PHRIT is a disarmingly simple yet powerful means of establishing anchors.

The more you use PHRIT, the more you will discover just how flexible it can be, both as an induction and as a framework for establishing all manner of conditioned connections.

EXERCISE

Practice using PHRIT as a self-hypnosis protocol.

In what ways does it differ from your practice of self-hypnosis?

If you do not usually practice self-hypnosis, consider experimenting with PHRIT, even if simply as a rapid relaxation tool.

When you are familiar with using PHRIT in this way, teach it to a friend or family member.

REVISITING HYPNOSIS

Trouble-Shooting and FAQ

Why not just use rapid inductions from the very beginning?

This has been addressed a number of times above. Essentially, PHRIT is an induction *and then some*.

If all you are only concerned with doing is getting someone into hypnosis as quickly as possible, then perhaps your time would be better spent solely concentrating on learning rapid or instant inductions. However, it is my view that an induction serves a bigger purpose.

You may want to read *The Anatomy of Inductions* for more.

Why can't you just use a slower induction to get someone into hypnosis and then just give a post-hypnotic suggestion for a rapid induction next time round?

As has been mentioned in part 1, prior to developing PHRIT, this was how I operated - and there is certainly nothing wrong with that. It is a useful way for a hypnotist to proceed gently in the first session. It is also an acceptable approach for Hypnotists who may lack the confidence to use rapid inductions from the beginning.

Nevertheless, since developing PHRIT, I have come to see that we do our clients a disservice if we treat inductions as merely a gateway into hypnosis. When used to their full potential, inductions can function as valuable and enjoyable learning experiences - and PHRIT provides an accessible framework for precisely that.

Again, you might want to get hold of a copy of *The Anatomy of Inductions* if you would like to explore this further.

What if they don't go as 'directly' the 3rd or 4th time and just stare back at me?

The very first time they don't respond, stop and find out why. It is possible that they may be intentionally blocking the process, for some unknown reason. Yet, in my experience, it is more likely that they did not fully understand what was expected of them.

Quite often it seems this happens if you skip from permissive to direct too early in the process - and they don't know how to do what you are asking of them.

There is no reason that you cannot repeat the first suggestion - that they take themselves back - more than once. This enables them to feel at ease with the process, ensures that they have learned what is required of them and increases the effect of the fractionation.

What was with all the anchoring and post-hypnotic suggestions discussion?

It's called value for money! At it's best, PHRIT is far more than an induction. It is a model for anchoring and post-hypnotic suggestions. Rather than simply provide you with a script for using PHRIT, we thought it would be useful to offer an explanation of how and why PHRIT works - and how it can be used as a framework for so much more.

Why do you keep talking about relaxation?

There is something of a disturbing trend amongst hypnotists at the moment to discredit relaxation. This seems to be a knee-jerk reaction to older models of hypnosis which define hypnosis as something like 'a state of relaxation.'

I do not believe that hypnosis can be completely equated with relaxation. That being said, I am yet to meet an effective therapist who did not appreciate the power of relaxation. Why would you not utilise that when you can?

When nearly half of all adults feel stressed every few days, with stress being the single biggest cause of visits to a GP surgery, I would be remiss if I did not offer my clients skills and experiences that can help them to relax.

Do you think Hypnosis is conditioning?

There are clearly elements of conditioning in Hypnosis, but there seems to be more involved as well.

This is a current area of academic debate and you can follow it by reading the works listed in the Recommended Reading section below.

In particular, I would recommend reading the work of Dr. Alfred Barrios.

So, if you don't think that Hypnosis is relaxation and you don't think that it is all conditioning, what is it?

This is dealt with more in *The Anatomy of Inductions*. In short, our understanding of hypnosis states that it is:

An imagination-fuelled, creatively engaged, shift in a person's perception of the world & their relationship to it.

Essentially, what we are talking about here is reframing things so effectively that our clients are enabled to imagine (and engage with) a new reality.

This is a thoroughly experiential model, which can not be fully explored at this point.

Do you repeat the PHRIT process in subsequent sessions?

There is no need to repeat the whole process after it has been taught. However, if there has been some delay from the previous session, I may briefly remind the client what they learned.

Alternatively, I may use the *Induction in its own right*

version from the previous section.

In the 'fuller' anchoring process, is that not just the NLP exercise known as stacking anchors?

This is a good question that is often asked in a number of different ways. And the answer is, "yes and no."

In the fuller anchoring process demonstrated in the 'Variations & Applications' section above, the strength of the anchor is increased each time it is fired. This can lead to some confusion.

It is important to note that the anchor is not intentionally or explicitly reinforced as and when it is fired. That is, we do not say to the client to squeeze their first to re-experience the confidence, whilst simultaneously squeezing their fist to anchor in the confidence they are currently feeling. This would confuse the client, muddy the waters and potentially neutralise the whole process.

However, we do offer the innocent suggestion that they may find that happening all by itself!

This is not 'stacking' anchors in the sense that we are not *explicitly* anchoring in e.g. increasing levels of confidence. Instead, it is an exercise in pacing and leading. We recognise that the fractionating effect of firing the anchor repeatedly in close succession may well have an exponential impact. Therefore, by suggesting the possibility of this, we imply that it is a hypnotic effect and generate greater confidence in the whole process.

What is the difference between Chaining Anchors, Stacking Anchors and Collapsing Anchors?

Collapsing anchors is the process of anchoring two different states - one negative and one positive. And both are fired at the same time, allowing the positive state to neutralise the negative.

Stacking anchors is the simple practice of anchoring more than one positive or resourceful state on top of another. This increases the power of the anchor.

Chaining anchors is a process whereby you create a link of anchors to move someone from an undesirable to state to a distant more positive state.

Couldn't you have said all of this in one page?

Yes! In fact, I could do better than that. I can say it all in just 4 lines:

1. You tell them to *do it* - "bring yourself back"

2. You tell them to *let it happen* - "allow yourself to come back"

3. You tell them *it can happen*, permissively - "you will find yourself..."

4. You tell them *it will happen*, directly - "you will come straight back"

EXERCISE

Continue to practice the PHRIT process, both as an induction and a framework for anchoring.

Consider any remaining questions that this book has brought up for you and ask them over at howtodoinductions.com

Or contact the author at briefhypnosis.com

Where Can I Learn More?

www.howtodoinductions.com

As you would expect, we would recommend our free inductions site as the premier website for learning about inductions.

Our web-site offers transcripts of various inductions, from the classics like Progressive Muscle Relaxations to the Bandler Handshake and the Leisure Induction. New inductions are added - and annotated - regularly, but only after they have been assessed as useful and achievable for beginners and experts alike.

www.briefhypnosis.com

Brief Hypnosis are the people behind *How to do inductions* and the *Inductions Masterclass* series of books.

Live Training

We also run live training in Solution-Focused

Hypnosis and Therapeutic Inductions, offering hands-on experience in creating inductions on-the-fly. You will learn principles and techniques that are not often taught elsewhere, which will take your confidence, creativity and client-base to new levels.

Sign-up for the newsletter at howtodoinductions.com to stay informed.

Recommended Reading

1. *How Hypnosis Happens: new cognitive theories of hypnotic responding* by Amanda J. Barnier, Zoltan Dienes, and Chris J. Mitchell

This is chapter 6 in the excellent Oxford Handbook of Hypnosis. Barnier, Dienes and Mitchell examine two models that may account for how hypnosis happens. These are Dienes and Perner's (2007) cold control theory of hypnosis and Barnier and Mitchell's (2005) discrepancy-attribution theory of hypnotic illusions.

2. *Executive Control Without Conscious Awareness: The cold control theory of hypnosis* - Zoltan Dienes & Josef Perner[12]

An interesting online article introducing the Cold Control Theory of Hypnosis. Although we do not push any particular model of hypnosis in this book, the Cold Control Theory does sit well with our discussion of Unconscious

12 http://www.lifesci.sussex.ac.uk/home/Zoltan_Dienes/cold %20control%20chapter.pdf

Learned Behaviours.

3. *Conditioned Reflex Therapy* by Andrew Salter

The classic book on assertiveness and conditioning that played a major role in the beginning of Behaviour Therapy.

Conditioned Reflex Therapy builds upon and expands Salter's earlier What is Hypnosis? which Theodore Barber declared "a work of genius". In this work, Salter further unpacks his theory that 'Hypnosis basically involves conditioned reactions and reflexes.'

4. *A Theory Of Hypnosis: An explanation of hypnotic induction, hypnotic phenomena, and post-hypnotic suggestion* By Alfred A. Barrios.[13]

Barrios offers a theory of hypnosis based mainly on principles of conditioning and inhibition.

The work of Dr. Barrios can be seen as a development of the Pavlovian model of Andrew Salter (recommended above). Reading Barrios' model alongside the Cold Control Theory put forward by Dienes and others is a profitable exercise sure to reward the reader.

5. *The Conditioning & Inhibition Theory of Hypnosis*

---

13 http://www.spccenter.com/theory_of_hypnosis.php

by Donald Robertson.[14]

Robertson presented a review of Barrios' position in the National Council for Hypnotherapy newsletter, contrasting it with the socio-cognitive model of Steven Jay Lynn.

6. *Hypnosis as Relaxation: Anesis* by William E. Edmonston Jr.

This is chapter 7 in Theories of Hypnosis, Edited by Steven J. Lynn and Judith W. Rhue. Edmonston argued that hypnosis and relaxation are "one and the same condition".

There are not many hypnotists today who would go that far. However, in light of the apparent rejection of relaxation amongst a number of up and coming new hypnotists, it would serve us well to consider Edmonston's detailed argument. After all, it may just be that although hypnosis is more than relaxation, the two function naturally and powerfully together.

7. *Monsters and Magical Sticks: Or, There's No Such Thing as Hypnosis* by Steven Heller and Terry Steele

If I could recommend only 1 book to new and/or experienced Hypnotists, it would be this. In fact, I would

---

14 http://www.hypnotherapists.org.uk/1104/july-research-snippet-competing-theories-of-hypnosis/

recommend this book to non-hypnotists just as quickly.

Heller demystifies the magic of hypnosis and argues that 'There is no such thing as hypnosis.' However, all is not as it seems. As Robert Anton Wilson is quoted as saying in the book, 'I've been practicing hypnosis all my life and didn't know it. And so have you!'

This book contains useful information on Anchoring.

8. *Frogs into Princes* by Richard Bandler and John Grinder

Written by NLP's co-founders, Frogs into Princes provides clear and practical information on Representation Systems, Reframing, Anchors and Anchoring.

EXERCISE

Continue to practice the PHRIT process.

This book can not guarantee that you will master PHRIT any more than a DVD on playing the Guitar can secure you a sell-out tour at Wembley Stadium.

Practice. Practice. Practice.

And then practice with a partner! Again and again and again...

And then practice some more.

APPENDIX A - Eliciting States

It may not be an exaggeration to write that the key to successful anchoring is strong state elicitation.

Generally speaking, the best states to anchor are naturally occurring states. You can usually trust that your clients will have had ample experience of entering these. The next most useful states for our purposes would often be past, vivid and highly associated states. The least preferable would be imagined, hypothetical or dissociated states. Having said that, if your goal is to grow as a practitioner and be flexible as a therapist, it is not a bad idea to practice until you are comfortable and competent with all three scenarios.

Before sharing a simple process to practice and learn from, I would like to briefly look at the difference between associated and dissociated states. You may have noticed in a couple of the transcripts, that we have used statements like "see what you saw". Additionally, a therapist might invite a client to "step into" their memory in order to relive aspects of the experience. These are all examples of associated states.

If I was assisting someone to reframe a troublesome memory, I might invite them to see it at a distance, or watch a video of themselves carrying out an action on a TV screen. This would be a dissociated state.

Generally, if I wanted someone to re-experience a state, I would have them do so from an associated perspective. I want them to step into it and really re-live it. However, if I was inviting them to consider it, perhaps more academically or to be able to describe it objectively, I would have them dissociate.

The Basic Process

1. Elect a State

Invite your client to think of a previous memory or experience of the state they wish to access. For example:

"Think of a time when you felt _____."

"Can you think of a specific example of _____?"

"When was the most recent time that you felt _____?"

"Can you remember a time when you were totally _____?"

If they do not have a personal example, you might use questions like:

"Do you know someone who is _____? Do you

ever wonder what that might feel like?"

"Do you know anyone who thinks or feels _____?"

"If you were the most _____ person on the planet, what do you think that might be like?"

2. Access the State

Associate into the state with your client.

"As you recall that experience, why don't you go ahead and step into that scene, step into your body and see what you saw, hear what you heard, and really feel the feelings of being totally _____."

"What would it be like if you were thinking or feeling _____, right now?"

As with the previous stage, if your client cannot think of a personal example, you can use questions like:

"What would it be like if you experienced that state for yourself? For example, what if you had a 'Freaky Friday' experience with someone who was totally _____?"

"Imagine witnessing the most _____ person on the planet... and stepping into their body. I wonder what it might feel like to be so _____ in the here and now?"

3. **Explore the state**

At this point, you want to assist your client to experience the state as fully as possible. Ask inviting, curious questions. The more they can discover here for themselves the better.

"I wonder what you might look like if you were _____? I wonder what that might feel like." [This question works as a useful link between the accessing stage and the exploration one.]

"What do you see? How big, bright, colourful, close, etc. is the image?"

"What do you hear, how clear, loud, close etc.?"

"What are you feeling? Where are those sensations in your body? How strong are they? Are they static or moving? What direction are they moving, etc.?"

"What would other people notice that was different about you? How would you explain to them what it felt like to be _____?"

"How are you standing when you are in that state? How do you walk, carry yourself, etc.?"

"What are you saying to yourself? What tone of voice, volume, and speed do you use in your internal dialogue?"

Many clients will not need this level of leading; they will simply and naturally explore these kind of questions for themselves. And you will find as you increase your skill at eliciting states that you can indirectly influence such exploration before they even get to this stage. However, it is useful to practice these questions and get adept at guiding your clients to as full an experience as possible.

If the memory or imagined scenario is not strong enough, you can intensify it by increasing the appropriate submodalities, or using as many representational systems as possible:

"And what is it like if you increase that feeling?"

"I wonder if you can notice the difference it makes if you make those colours brighter?"

"What is the effect of turning down that sound... and now increasing it?"

"What happens if you double that? What does that look like? And how does it feel?"

4. **Evaluate the State**

This step is not always followed by practitioners, but

it can be invaluable. Here you clarify the essential aspects of the state. What is it about the memory or experience they are thinking of that is going to be helpful for them? What is the exact nature of that help?

"What about this state captures the essence of it for you?"

"What about this state makes it distinct from all other states for you?"

"How will feeling this way be useful for you?"

This stage can occur both before or after exploration and intensification of the state.

APPENDIX B - Stacking Anchors

Stacking anchors is a relatively simple process to strengthen a positive anchor. In essence, you anchor more than one positive state to the same trigger.

The states chosen can be the same, or different. If you are seeking to anchor a general resourceful state, you can stack different states to the same trigger. For example, you might stack Confident on top of Motivated, on top of Powerful, on top of Energetic. And so on.

Alternatively, if you are seeking to strengthen a very specific state - perhaps one of the stepping-stones used in chaining anchors - then you would aim, to elicit difference instances of the same state.

- Elicit an instance of the state you wish to anchor.

- Anchor the state

- Break state and test

- Continue steps 1-3

- Break State

- Test the completed stack

APPENDIX C - Chaining Anchors

Chaining anchors is a process used to enable someone to travel from an undesirable state to a more resourceful state. At times, the distance between those two states may appear too far for someone to jump in one leap. (Whether this is true, or merely the perception of the person you are working with, is mostly irrelevant.) In such circumstances, Chaining Anchors is a valuable tool to use.

Essentially, you create a path of stepping-stones to enable someone to progress through states that appear to be polar opposites.

To begin, you will want to establish the client's current state, or the state that they wish to move out of. You will then need to clarify where it is that they wish to get to. For example, they may want to travel from "terrified" to "on top of the world".

Once you have your current or unwanted state, you then ask the client to think of what they would need to get out of that state. In NLP terms, this is an *away-from* move, which is a more achievable step for those who feel stuck in some state or circumstance. Once there, you ask for a *towards* step. Then finally, you have them move from this third state to their desired state.

The steps below outline the Chaining Anchors process.

1. Anchor negative state. Break state.

2. Anchor away-from state. Break state.

3. Anchor towards state. Break state.

4. Anchor desired state. Break state.

5. Test each trigger. Break state after each test.

6. Link the chain:

- Fire first trigger. Just as reaching peak, also:
- Fire second trigger. Then let go of first, and:
- Fire third trigger. Then let go of second, and:
- Fire fourth trigger and then let go of third.

7. Break state.

8. Test chain by firing first trigger. Break state.

9. Future pace.

That may all seem rather convoluted, so here's a transcript of the technique in practice:

Hypnotist: "So, we've been talking about Kick-boxing. And this is something you want to get back into. And you know it's good for you, you can feel it's good for you - and you enjoy it. What a great combination!

"And when you do go, when there's no stopping you, what's that feeling? What's the feeling you need to get to that would guarantee you go to Kick-boxing as often as you want?"

Client: "When I'm really into it, I feel buzzed. It's like, it's like my whole body is revved-up and there's no stopping me."

H: "Buzzed? Ok, that's great.

"And we've been hearing that it doesn't always work out as planned. Tell me a bit about that."

C: "I just get in after work and even though that morning I was determined to go, it's like it has drained away. It honestly feels like I couldn't go if my life depended on it! I have zero energy for it."

H: "Okay, so after work, when you've maybe been drained, isn't working for you. So, what would be a more realistic time for you to go Kick-boxing. I'm not asking when you'd like to, or when you feel you should. I'm asking, if you look into the future and see yourself kick-boxing, when is that most likely to be happening."

C: "In the morning, on a Thursday."

H: "They have sessions then?"

C: "Yeah, twice a week."

H: "Okay, so we already know one way to increase your chances of going. Stop trying to go after work and go first thing on a Thursday!"

C: "Sorted!" [Laughs.]

H: "But sometimes, even on a Thursday, you don't go. What's that about?"

C: "It's weird. It's as if I wake up with the end-of the day feeling. You know? I could wake up full of energy, but the minute I think about going to kick-boxing, I immediately get that drained feeling."

H: "Okay, and how would you describe that feeling?"

C: "It's like... [Sighs, as drops shoulders]... Like I'm slumped down in the chair. I feel flat and 'flumped'."

H: "Flumped?"

C: "Yeah."

H: "So, shall we use that word to describe that state? Flumped?"

C: "Sure. Yeah."

H: "Okay, so do your best to get back that flat, flumped feeling. That even-though-it's-a-thursday-morning-I-just-can't-be-arsed feeling... Get a real sense for it in your mind, but also get that physical flat, flumped, feeling. Give me a nod when you can recreate that now."

C: [Nods.]

H: [Touches knuckle of first finger.] "That's great.

"Ok. So..." [Removes finger.]

[Breaks State:]

"How many people generally go to the kick-boxing classes?"

C: "Oh, it varies. In the morning, might only be 3 or 4. But Monday nights you can get 20 or 30."

H: "Wow, that's a lot."

C: "Yeah."

H: "It's a popular class then?"

C: "Yeah, very."

H: "So, what do you think it would take to move you from on from 'Flumped'? What feeling or state could move you out of that?

"And, if it helps, you can think of a time when you actually have progressed away from 'flumped'."

C: "Oh, easy. It's frustrated. I get annoyed at myself and how silly I'm being."

H: "And that works for you?"

C: "Yeah. If anyone else did it, I'd get stubborn. But when I nag myself it works!" [Laughs.]

H: [Laughs.] "I hear you! So, okay, we'll go with Frustrated. Can you remember a time when you felt frustrated in that way?"

C: "Yeah."

H: "Okay. Think of a specific time when you felt frustrated. And I want you to really feel it now. See what you saw. Hear what you heard. *Feel what you felt.*"

C: [Closes eyes.]

H: "That's it. And when you've really got it, nod your head to let me know."

C: [Nods head.]

H: [Touches knuckle of second finger.] "Excellent. Really frustrated." [Lets go of knuckle.]

"Have you seen the Van Damme film, 'Kickboxer'?"

C: "Yeah. Awful!" [Laughs.]

H: "It really was! [Laughs.] But I think back then there were so few decent martial arts films, that you kinda just took what you could get."

C: "Oh, totally."

H: "Now, tell me, what would you need to get from Frustrated to Buzzed?"

C: "Determination. That feeling of, I'm fucking

doing this!"

H: "Gotcha. So the state we are moving on to, to get you from Frustrated to Buzzed is Determined?"

C: "Yeah, definitely."

H: "Okay. And can you remember a time when you were determined? Remember a specific time."

C: "Yeah. Got one."

H: "Ok, so *really* feel that. *Really* feel determined. Get into that feeling, into that state. See what you saw, hear what you heard and feel what you felt."

C: [Stares out in front of himself, eyes glazed.]

H: "And when you are really feeling that, that peak of Determined, nod your head to let me know."

C: [Nods head.]

H: [Touches third knuckle.] "That's it. [Lets go.]

"So, why did you choose Kick-boxing, rather than regular boxing?"

C: "Well, I came from Martial Arts, so it was a natural move. I like kicking and sweeping and stuff."

H: "Cool.

"Well, finally, I'd like you to think of a time when you were just Buzzed. I mean, you're unstoppable. Your whole body is just revved-up."

C: [Nods head.]

H: "You've got one already? Ok, let's go with that then. And really get into that state. Get that buzzed sensation all over. Just completely no stopping you.

"And when you've got that, go ahead and nod your head."

C: [Nods head.]

H: "Good. Now really feel that... [Touches fourth knuckle.] Good work." [Lets go.]

C: "That feels great!"

H: "Yeah?"

C: "Yeah, I feel like going for a jog or

something!"

H: "Excellent! But before we do that, can you think of the first album you bought?"

C: "Um, I think it was *Bad* by Michael Jackson."

H: "Really? Ok, now can you notice what happens when I fire off this anchor here..." [Touches first knuckle.]

C: [Nods.]

H: "What's that like?"

C: "It's that slumped in the chair feeling."

H: "Mine was *Thriller*. Great album."

C: "Yeah, much better than his others!"

H: "And notice this..." [Touches second knuckle.]

C: "Ha. I can feel it!"

H: "What?"

C: "The frustration."

H: "Great. Do you remember the game, 'Frustration'?"

C: "With the dice in the little dome?"

H: "And you pushed it down to flip the dice."

C: "Yeah, it was one of our rainy day games."

H: "Same here.

"And now what happens when I touch this knuckle?" [Touches third knuckle]

C: "Yep. [Nods head.] Yep. That determination. I can feel it building."

H: "Perfect. Have you done this before?"

C: "No."

H: "But you've been hypnotised before?"

C: "Yeah, I made out with a broom on stage!" [Laughs.]

H: [Laughs.] "Hey, there's no judgement here!

"So, notice what happens now..." [Touches fourth knuckle.]

C: "Yeah, I can feel it." [Nods head enthusiastically.]

H: "Buzzed?"

C: "Totally buzzed!"

H: "So you didn't do the whole cluck like a chicken thing then?"

C: "Nah. Well, not that I remember!"

H: "Right, all that's left to do now is link these up. You ready?"

C: "Sure."

H: [Touches first knuckle. Then, as the peak is being reached, simultaneously touches second knuckle and then removes finger from first knuckle. As peak is being reached on the second knuckle, also touches third knuckle and then removes finger from second knuckle. As peak is being reached on the third knuckle, also touches fourth knuckle and then removes finger from third knuckle.]

C: [Nods head.]

H: "I don't think Bad was a lousy album, but it was definitely downhill from there."

C: "Yeah."

H: "I had Thriller on LP. This big double-LP with

a picture of Jacko on the front laying down with Tiger cubs. It was my prized possession!"

C: "Do you still have it?"

H: "Sadly, no. And I have no idea what happened to it.

"Anyway, let's check that chain! Notice what happens now." [Touches first knuckle for a number of seconds.]

C: [Nods head and smiles.] "Well, that works!"

H: "Talk me through it."

C: "I could just feel this shift. Like a progression. And it was like I was just getting a handle on one feeling when it was moving on to the next. And I was left with a nice buzz!"

H: "Sound good to me."

C: "Definitely!"

H: "Tell me, you know a bit about NLP... What's the difference between a State-break and a pattern-interrupt?"

C: [Thinks for a few seconds...] "I guess sometimes..."

H: "You know what? There's no time for that.

"So, do me a favour and travel to a future Thursday morning and tell me about the 'flumped'..."

C: [Laughs.] "I can't get it!"

H: "You can't feel flumped?"

C: [Shakes head.] "Nope."

H: "Are you really trying?"

C: [Laughs.] "I really am. The minute you said go to a future Thursday, I was trying to feel the way I feel, but it's not there. I just wanna get up and go Kick-boxing!"

Bibliography

Andreas, S. (1994) NLP: *The New Technology of Achievement*. New York: William Morrow.

Bandler, R & Grinder, J. (1981). *Trance-formations: Neurolinguistic Programming and the Structure of Hypnosis*. Utah: Real People Press.

Bandler, R & Grinder, J. (1979). *Frogs into Princes*. Utah: Real People Press.

Barnier, A.J. (2001). "Posthypnotic Suggestion: Attention, Awareness and Automaticity". *Sleep and Hypnosis*, 1:57-63.

Barrios, A. (2009). *Understanding Hypnosis: Theory, Scope and Potential*. New York: Nova Science Publishers, Inc.

Gilligan, S. G. (1987). *Therapeutic Trances*. New York: Routledge.

Hall, Michael L. (2004). *Sourcebook of Magic: A Comprehensive Guide to NLP Change Patterns*. Carmarthen, Wales: Crown House Publishing

Hall, Michael L. (1999). *The User's Manual for the Brain*. Carmarthen, Wales: Crown House Publishing

Heller, S & Steele, T. (1987). *Monsters and Magical Sticks: Or, There's No Such Thing as Hypnosis*. Carmarthen, Wales: Crown House Publishing

Hassin, R., Uleman, J., & Bargh, J., eds. (2005). *The New Unconscious*. Oxford: OUP.

Nongard, R. (2007). *Inductions and Deepeners: Styles and Approaches for Effective Hypnosis*. Andover, KS: Peach Tree Professional Education.

Lynn, S. & Rhue, J. Eds. (1991) *Theories of Hypnosis: Current Models and Perspectives*. New York: Guilford Press.

Nash, M. & Barnier, A., eds. (2008). *The Oxford Handbook of Hypnosis: Theory, Research, and Practice*. Oxford: OUP.

Old, G. (2014). *Mastering the Leisure Induction*. Milton Keynes: 61 Books.

Overdurf, J & Silverthorn, J. (1995). *Training Trances*. Portland, OR: Metamorphouos.

Tiers, M. (2010). *Integrative Hypnosis*. USA: Melissa Tiers.

Salter, A. (1949). *Conditioned Reflex Therapy: The Direct Approach To The Reconstruction Of Personality*. New York: Creative Age Press.

Salter, A. (1973). *What is Hypnosis? Studies in Conditioning*. New York: Farrar Straus Giroux.

Vaknin, S. (2011). *The Big Book of NLP Techniques*. USA: Inner Patch Publishing.

About the Author

Graham Old is a Solution-focused Hypnotist from the United Kingdom. A Graduate of Spurgeon's College, London and the University of Wales, Graham is a former University Chaplain and remains an active participant of local peace and justice campaigns. He also has experience as a Father's Worker and Assistant Social Worker, as well as working in private practice and running the most popular inductions site on the web.

Graham is a popular conference speaker, writer and trainer, with two decades experience teaching meditation and self-hypnosis. He is an innovative presence in contemporary hypnosis and the developer of the popular Therapeutic Inductions approach.